The Beginning Artist's Survival Guide: How to Turn your Artwork into Prints
by William Toliver

Published by WHTART, LLC

433 Belle Grove Dr
Richardson, Tx 75083

WHTART.net

Copyright © 2021 by William Toliver

All rights reserved. No portion of this book may be reproduced in any form without permission from the publisher, except as permitted by U.S. copyright law. For permissions contact: Contact@whtart.net

Cover by William Toliver.

HI I'M WILLIAM TOLIVER, AN ARTIST LOCATED IN THE DFW AREA. FOR THE PAST 5 YEARS I'VE BEEN SELLING MY WORK AND WANTED TO SHARE WHAT I'VE LEARNED WITH YOU, THE BEGINNING ARTIST.

You've just finished your latest masterpiece, now what? Have you ever thought about selling prints of your work while you wait for the original to sell?

My friend, *Goob*, will show you **How to Turn Your Artwork into Prints** in 3 easy steps!

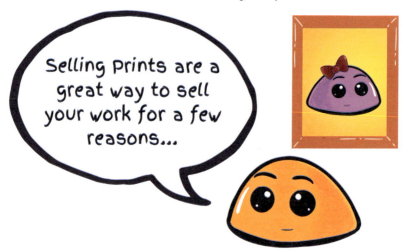

Selling prints are a great way to sell your work for a few reasons...

4 Advantages of Selling Prints

- **Passive Income** - prints bring in continuous sales
- **Accessibility** - prints allow people to invest/collect your work even if they can't buy an original
- **Versatile** - prints can come in a range of sizes, shapes, alternative colors, and can be *hand-embellished*
- **Everlasting** - prints will not fade over time

*Hand-embellished is when an artist applies their unique touch with their particular art medium to a print

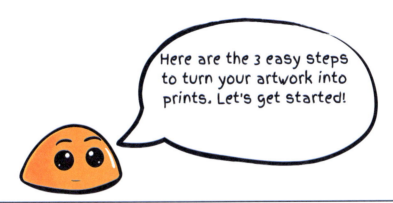

Step 1: Digitizing your Artwork (Scanned/Photographed)

- *I would recommend that you take your artwork to your local fine art printing company to get professionally scanned or photographed.*

3 reasons why you should get your work professionally digitized
1. They will have equipment that can handle artwork of all sizes.
2. They will know how to work with paintings of various mediums and on different materials.
3. They will know how to capture all of the details that you've put into your work.

We do not want blurry prints do we? This is where **DPI** comes into play.

Step 1: Digitizing your Artwork (Scanned/Photographed)

What is **DPI**?

DPI (dots per inch) is the number of dots that can be placed in a line across one inch. The higher the DPI, the sharper the image.

There are 3 ranges of DPI settings that you need to know

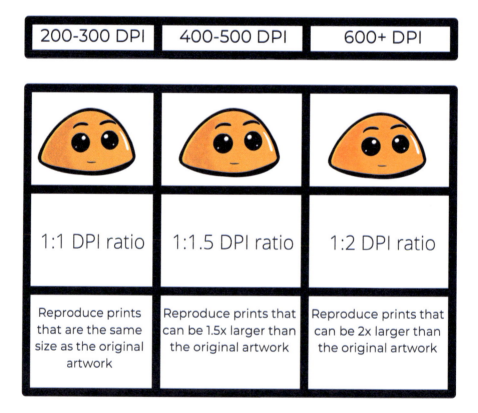

Helpful Tip

- When getting your work digitized you want to use a resolution setting of at least 300 DPI.

Step 2: Color Correcting your Digitized Artwork

When you get your artwork digitized the new file will be in **RGB** (red, blue, green) color format .
- The RGB color format is commonly used *for digital products, webpages, etc.*

Although *for physical/professional prints* most printing companies use a **CYMK** (cyan, yellow, magenta, black) color format.

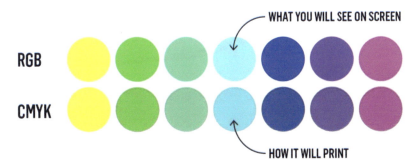

As you can see, the CYMK colors are not as vibrant and lacks the range of colors that the RGB colors do.

Step 2: Color Correcting your Digitized Artwork

3 options to color correct your digitized artwork for printing

- *Easiest Option* - Find a printing company that specializes in printing artwork
    - most likely they will have a graphic designer in house that can help you (this will cost extra)
    - more expensive option
- **Favorite Option** - Work with a freelance graphic designer to color correct your image
- **Hardest Option** - use photoshop to color correct the image yourself
    - saves money
    - time consuming and frustrating if you don't know how to use photoshop well

BEFORE I FORGET, THIS GOLDEN RULE WILL SAVE YOU TIME AND MONEY.

GOLDEN RULE: ALWAYS GET SAMPLES DONE BEFORE YOU ORDER PRINTS.

Step 3: Printing Your Work

> Once you get your samples the way you like, IT'S TIME TO PRINT.

Step 3: Printing Your Work

> NOW THAT YOU HAVE A DIGITIZED COPY OF YOUR ARTWORK, AND COLORED CORRECTED IT. YOU HAVE AN IMPORTANT DECISION TO MAKE...

WHICH PAPER DO YOU PRINT ON?

This a personal preference by the artist.
- The quality/look of your prints will look different on each type of paper
    - Glossy Prints
        - *Pros*:
            - High glare finish
            - Highly colorful/intense
        - *Cons*:
            - Viewing angle can reduce the print's visibility
            - Lighting can cause a glare
    - Satin Prints (*my favorite print type*)
        - *Pros*:
            - Full color capability of the gloss/high resolution
            - Less affected by viewing angle
            - Better suited for displaying images behind glass
    - Matte Prints
        - *Pros*:
            - No reflective surface
        - *Cons*:
            - Lacks color range/dull colors

Step 3: Printing Your Work

Remember the Golden Rule:
ALWAYS GET SAMPLES DONE BEFORE YOU ORDER PRINTS.

A few quick tips and resources before you go...

3 Print Sizing Tips

1. To help you figure out whether to scale your artwork up or down proportionally, use the app **Aspect Ratio x Calculator**.
2. Make your prints into easily framable sizes for your customers
   - *For example*: 4x6, 8x10, 11x14, 18x24 etc
3. Place a small .5" inch border around each image so customers do not need to mat your prints when they get framed.

Local Resource List

PRINT SHOPS | LOCATION

Precision Reprographics — Dallas
Coupralux (Specializes in Fine Art) — Dallas
Miller Imaging and Digital Solutions — Austin
Thomas Printworks — Multiple Locations

Art Term Bank

- *Limited Edition Print*-artists restrict the total amount of artworks produced in the edition, so that each individual work will retain its value over time.
    - **Pro tip**: When selling limited editions they are often sold in number order. If there is a lot of demand for the edition, you may choose to raise the price of the remaining unsold works. In these cases, the print numbered 30/30 will be more expensive than the print numbered 1/30—simply because it was the last to be sold.
- *Open Edition Print*-is a print that has no limit to the number printed. They are not numbered nor signed usually, unlike limited edition prints.
- *Giclee Print*-is made using pigment-based inks and produce the sharpest detail and highest resolution, displaying a full-color spectrum of your artwork
    - **Pro tip**: Inkjet printers use dye-based inks and might not capture all of your artwork's details
- *Hand Embellished Print*-is when an artist applies their unique touch with their particular art medium to a print.

Navigating this new world of trying to sell your work as a beginning artist is very difficult. That is why I created this survival guide. There are so many things you have to do: pricing, marketing, monitoring expenses, finding time to create... the list goes on. I wanted to create a guide to help ease some of the burdens we all face. This will be the first part of compiling the knowledge I have gained over the years as an artist. I hope this guide will help save you lots of
time, money, and stress.

-Will

"Atlantis" — Watercolor

"Exchange" — Mixed Media

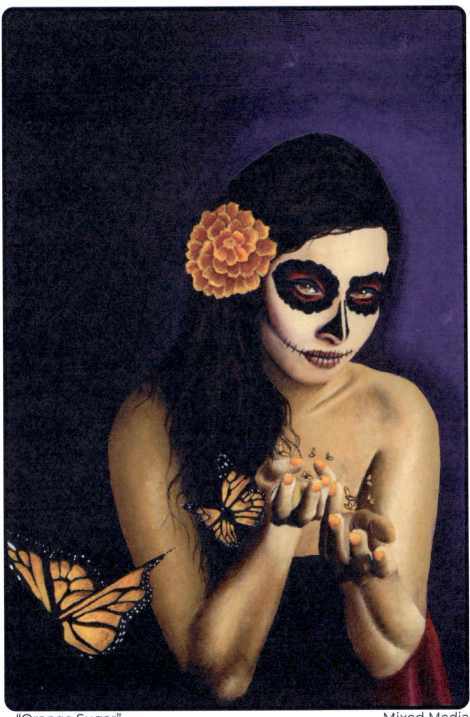

"Orange Sugar" — Mixed Media

"Rose" — Pencil

"Blue Eyes" — Watercolor

"Day 87" — Acrylic

"Luna & Double U" — Acrylic

"Hear No Evil" — Mixed Media

"You" — Mixed Media

"Cottoncandi" — Acrylic

"Nebula" — Acrylic

"Lyric" — Acrylic

"Truth" Acrylic

"Enough" — Acrylic